FOREWORD

Since 1991, here at Young Writers we have celebrated the awesome power of creative writing, especially in young adults where it can serve as a vital method of expressing their emotions and views about the world around them. In every poem we see the effort and thought that each student published in this book has put into their work and by creating this anthology we hope to encourage them further with the ultimate goal of sparking a life-long love of writing.

Our latest competition for secondary school students, **The Power of Poetry,** challenged young writers to consider what was important to them and how to express that using the power of words. We wanted to give them a voice, the chance to express themselves freely and honestly, something which is so important for these young adults to feel confident and listened to. They could give an opinion, highlight an issue, consider a dilemma, impart advice or simply write about something they love. There were no restrictions on style or subject so you will find an anthology brimming with a variety of poetic styles and topics. We hope you find it as absorbing as we have.

We encourage young writers to express themselves and address subjects that matter to them, which sometimes means writing about sensitive or contentious topics. If you have been affected by any issues raised in this book, details on where to find help can be found at
www.youngwriters.co.uk/info/other/contact-lines

THE POWER OF POETRY

BULLYING

ENVIRONMENT

EQUALITY

YOUR FUTURE

HOPE

CHANGE

CONFLICT

YOUR DREAMS

IDENTITY

WORDS OF WONDER

EDITED BY DEBBIE KILLINGWORTH

First published in Great Britain in 2023 by:

 Young**Writers**

Young Writers
Remus House
Coltsfoot Drive
Peterborough
PE2 9BF
Telephone: 01733 890066
Website: www.youngwriters.co.uk

Printed and bound in the UK by BookPrintingUK
Website: www.bookprintinguk.com
YB0MA0040A

CONTENTS

Isabelle Fratson (13) 39
Henry Sans Johnson (13) 40
Cherry Austin (13) 41
Reagan Jarvis-Shaw (13) 42

Cove School, Cove

Caleb Tamale-Sali (12) 43

Cromwell Community College, Chatteris

Amy Cole (14) 44
Tilly Boniface (14) 46

Danesfield CE School, Williton

Erin Ramsey (12) 47

Danetre And Southbrook Learning Village, Daventry

Lexie Carvell (14) 48
Jayden Rushton (12) 50
Maggie-May Jalland-Baker (12) 51
Fearne Badger (12) 52
Xavier Deka (13) 53
Henry Bendall (13) 54
Helen Loc (14) 55
Olivia Nawrocka (13) 56
Mason Baker (14) 57
Evie Jones (13) 58
Elianna Wojnicki (11) 59
Alisha Barber (12) 60
Joseph Howells (11) 61
Giulia Cirja (12) 62
Ethan Williams-Marsh (13) 63
Jack Retief (12) 64
Cyran Davies (12) 65
Jacob Hines (12) 66
Leilani Albert (12) 67
Charlie Cullinane (12) 68

Ecclesfield School, Sheffield

Mia Holt-Barker (13) 69
Kira Green (11) 70
Ebony Hanson (13) 72
Phoebe Clayton 73
Elina Pym (11) 74

Eden Boys Leadership Academy East, Birmingham

Rayan Ali (12) 75
Mohamed El Bikry (14) 76

Gairloch High School, Gairloch

Kealan Mackenzie (14) 77

Golspie High School, Golspie

Aine Martin (15) 78
Lexie Macleod (14) 80

Hall Green School, Hall Green

Alisha Lone (14) 82

Horizon Community College, Barnsley

Chelsie Quinn (12) 84
Andreea Nita (13) 85

Hornchurch High School, Hornchurch

Ibrahim Yusuf (12) 86
Sydney Allsopp (11) 87
Teddy Scott (14) 88

Macmillan Academy, Middlesbrough

Ned Rowcroft (12) 89
Cobie-Sharon Harrison (12) 90
Anna Pearson (12) 91

Wellingborough School, Wellingborough

Liam Dickinson (12)	128
Harrison Gillard (12)	130
Henry Summerfield (12)	131

West Buckland School, Barnstaple

Meredith Marcolini (13)	132

THE
POEMS

ADHD And Me

If you don't mind, I'd like to tell you about a little thing
called ADHD
and how it affects my brain
it can make me go hypo
lash out
and not concentrate
but it doesn't stay in my head
It displays in my body and it takes me a little while to
process the feeling
a girl struggling is what you can see
I lash out at the littlest things
clicking pens
ticking clocks
I try to fit in but I come across as rude
my control fades
I dance, sing, dance, scream and shout
and show embarrassing, intense emotions
all trapped inside my head
It's not just embarrassing, silly and stupid
it's a part of me
and a lot of people
I've just not got a typical brain
I'm Maisy, I am me
Please see through my label of ADHD.

Maisy Aldred

Story Of My Life

My hair was as golden as the sun,
Yet darker than the depths of the ocean,
The freckles scattered over my face,
Like litter in a school,
My raging blue eyes drew attention to people
But the green is what drove them away,
Or was it the scar
Which I tried covering with pictures of aliens I
saw in my sleep.

The way I dressed wasn't much better,
Some days it would be joggers and jumpers,
Others it was short, cropped T-shirts.
My favourite was a slightly cropped hoodie with a zipper.
It was a pillow holding me tight.
But I wouldn't let anyone change who I was or what I was.

Iggy Taylor

Save Our World

The world is full of creatures big and small
Some are long, some are strong and some are even tall.
However, there are some negatives
Like pollution that is getting out of control
There may not be a solution
There is a range of climate change ruining our world
Deforestation
Trees gone
Wildlife being destroyed
Deforestation is ruining our planet
Please stop
We don't want any more of the wildlife to drop.
We want
Flowers blooming
Animals breeding
And last of all...
The sun beaming.

Adelina Todd

Scarfell Roads

On the path up to the peak
the clouds enveloped us
our visibility stripped from our weary eyes
a path of hidden doors upon us
following the crowd we arrive at the peak.
After our eyes had been exposed to the views from the
throne of England
we departed down a clear mountain past a few people.
Before we know it the clouds had enveloped us once again
and led us down a rocky track to a ledge cleared of fog
with the greatest view we had ever seen.
Often the worst roads lead to the greatest places.

Noah Barratt

I'm Great

I can't remember the last time someone asked me if I was
okay
And I don't mean in a superficial way

Like taking the time to drop by
Whilst I'm home for the day
And stay for a bit

I've been in school three hours
And still no one has said hello

I think people assume I'm fine
Because I make them smile
I make them feel a certain way
By asking, "Are you okay?"
And if they ask how I am
I say, "I'm great."

Jessica Thompson

Celebrating Love

Love is a frozen lake,
You walk across with another.
They can sabotage the ice,
Or they can walk across with you.

I walked across with you.
Our souls interlocked,
Our fingers entwined,
Our love confined.

How can we love each other,
When others don't love us,
When we aren't accepted?
We have been intercepted.

Fear and judgment,
Tore us apart.
But now stronger than ever,
We can restart.

Kaiyah Hussey (16)

Ukraine On The Run

Ukraine on the run, Ukraine on the run,
Russia has all the power,
There is no more fun,
Only bloodshed and Ukrainians going down under,
There is no escape,
Russia will eventually get what they want,
Buildings being destroyed, just like grapes,
NATO pleading, saying don't,
Bodies all around, decay,
There's no need for innocent people to die,
It's like this every day,
Soldiers saying goodbye.

Lewie Currington

The World Is Dying

Rainforests are being cut down
Orangutans losing their homes
The world is dying

Ice caps are starting to melt
Polar bears are starving
The world is dying

The sky is being polluted
Nature is being destroyed
The world is dying

We are killing the land around us
We need to stop
We are as dangerous as murderers
The world is dying.

Ihsan Shariff

All The Fallen Soldiers

All the fallen soldiers
So peaceful on the ground
They're all as still as soldiers
None of them make a sound

Though they are dead, they're present
Inside my head they feast
They ought to haunt my mind
A guilty mindless beast

The army's brutal battalion
They are all I see
The running of a stallion
The redness of the sea.

Elliott Jay

Moon

The wind rose from the west;
grey clouds. The extinct ocean
covered the sky. Can you see
through the thin fog? Like being
carried away by the waves.
Shuttle flies golden?
Here he disappeared... Flashed...
now he disappeared behind the wave
here again he swam up and shines.

Oleksandra Hanzilevska

Winston

W inston is a dog, he loves to run
 I n the pool he is very fast
N o one has a dog like Winston
S ometimes he barks for hours
T reat time is his favourite
O nly Winston jumps into the bushes!
N o one loves Winston like me.

Milo McGhee

Animal Cruelty

A nimals are an important part of our lives
N othing, people are doing for these poor creatures
I n fact, all they're doing is looking at their features
M ainly they're cute coloured fur or tail
A nd they also sadly always fail
L ike when humans hurt them and test products on them

C uts and bruises used with knives
R uining our animals' lives
U nfortunately, this is what happens on the planet
E very innocent little animal getting hurt
L ikely always get hit
T o all the people in France
Y ou will never get a second chance.

Lola Faulkner-Lote (12)

Aldridge School, Aldridge

Racism In Football

Every year there is a lot that happens
When football comes around
Sometimes there is racial abuse
That gives some players a frown
When some players miss the net
The fans give them a snap
Then they will all feel sad
And a player will give them a tap

During Euro 2020, in the final game
Some England players missed
That made them feel ashamed
Saka, Rashford, Sandcho
As well had to get some tissues
After being attacked by fans
By being racially abused

We all need to stop this
It's getting out of hand
Or players will be getting upset
And they'll be crying in the sand.

Alex Bullock (12)
Aldridge School, Aldridge

Animal Cruelty

A nimals get hurt because of our actions
N ot tomorrow, not later... now
I believe this should never have begun
M aking animal cruelty stop is the dream
A iming to finish this monstrosity
L iving the life of being poked around

C ould it ever be stopped for good?
R ace for time to stop this going any further
U nder the bright light every day
E veryone can pitch in to help
L eave them alone
T est after test, they never think about how the animals feel
Y es, this event is happening.

Hannah White (11)
Aldridge School, Aldridge

Climate

C an we save our planet?

L et's make shelters for those who are homeless so they don't get wet by rainstorms or other disasters

I t's our responsibility to make sure our crops get enough rain to grow

M ake sure people aren't dehydrated and get enough water because of heatwaves and hot temperatures

A nd people should offer to create shelter for storms

T rees should be planted for oxygen

E veryone should care or we will be in great danger.

Malaika Bashir (12)

Aldridge School, Aldridge

Football

F ootball is a beautiful game
O nly if there is no racism
O f course, there is racism
T o football because it is a large sport
B est footballers can be racist
A lso Sergio Busquets' act
L eft him with a lot of hate
L eave the act of racism and enjoy the beautiful game.

Kwame Bediako (12)

Aldridge School, Aldridge

Rain

Rain! Rain everywhere
Rain! It was soaking my hair
I washed it this morning
But the rain won't stop falling

I had to have cottage pie for dinner
I'm so not a winner
I wasn't allowed pudding
And now my house is flooding
Rain!

Maddison Bottomer (12)
Aldridge School, Aldridge

Accept The Exceptions

Miss Cool,
I'm that clown,
Who's always down,
The infamous Miss Cool,
That sleeps in school,
I can't help that so
Accept that!

IDK Guy,
I don't know what am I?
A boy or girl?
I don't know if I belong in this world,
Well doesn't seem I'll ever know,
But that's just me so,
Accept that!

Mr Insecure,
Am I too tall,
Is my voice too deep,
I feel backed against a wall,
Wondering about all my issues in my sleep,
Yeah, that's me,
Accept that!

Miss Rebel,
I can't stand it,
All the injustice,

Like never-ending brutal hits,
With that, I'll still get my point through without Miss,
I'll protest proudly so,
Accept that!

Miss Clever,
Yep, pi divided by 2 equals 1.57,
Another right answer to add to the previous 11,
I passed all of my test,
Yeah, I know I'm the absolute best,
Now if you don't mind but,
Accept that.

Mr Know It All,
Your wrong I'm right,
I'll prove it in a fight,
Of debate that is,
I'm sure I'll win this,
Obviously, you should,
Accept that!

Accept who we are,
Accept what we are,
Accept when we're here,
Accept why we're here,
Accept where we're from,
Accept us,
Accept us for our views,

Accept us how we are,
Accept us for what we love,
Accept us all as exceptions!
Accept the exceptions!

Phoebe Haastrup (13)
Alec Hunter Academy, Braintree

Daddy Isn't Coming Home

Dear children,
As the grass I lay upon becomes the deathbed of the mates
I once bestowed the honour to learn of you,
They carry your memory to the grave.
Although I'm not here, know I'm always near.
Daddy's here to wipe your tears.
Our governments are fickle; we're puppets in a sick game of torment.
We bat our balls towards the enemy and leave with half our men on the bench,
If I don't make this out breathing, don't fear, don't cry,
Because the chances are increasing that I'll make it out alive,
We're steadily on our way to achieving victory,
A war to end all wars will go down in history,
However, I still find myself wondering where the line is drawn between life and death,
And was all this really worth it,
If I just end up dead?

Chloe Dyson (15)
All Saints Catholic High School, Sheffield

The Sky's Trees

I love to dwell in forest wild, where looming pine trees pierce the clouds.
A beauty where nature smiled, a fitting place to live and die;
Have you ever really looked at the pretty sky and maybe seen its perfect beauty?
You could learn that the sky's trees know your protection is a stern and sacred duty.
Protection of that which is spreading their long lives through tails of ordinate patterns,
Trees though many summers grown,
safeguarding of those temples of green,
where the song of birds is known.

Make a change for our world
before the days unwind,
look after the bees and don't scare our trees.

Cora Colledge (13)
All Saints Catholic High School, Sheffield

Bullying Isn't Okay!

B ullying isn't okay! Other kids shouldn't be each others' prey.

U nderaged children shouldn't be bullied by an older age.

L ike it or not, don't bully others! It's not fair, people are backing down.

L earn to stick up for yourself! And be brave, don't give up, and show them what you can do.

Y ou and your friends should be a team and go around to warn others!

I , myself, have been bullied but I got through it! Just ignore. You'll be okay.

N obody should be in this situation. It's not nice and that should be taught.

G o help others if you see someone who can't do anything and tell them, "You're the bigger person!" Now I've told you, go be that helpful person for me!

Lacie-Jade Law (12)

Archbishop Sentamu Academy, Hull

Ukraine's Hope

They have been through a lot,
Russia has tied Ukraine in a knot.
How they cope,
Is with their hope.
Even though they are stuck in a rope,
All the countries have hope.
Ukraine has been through pain,
But Russia has no brain,
So it means Ukraine will reign.
War is poor,
And there is so much gore.
But as long as war is here,
We won't cheer.
Ukraine will pull through
Against the big bull!

Ethan Overton-Braesyde (14)
Baston House School, Hayes

A Piano Poem

I like music
I like pop music
It makes me feel happy
It makes me feel excited

I like my piano
It makes me feel calm
It has black and white keys
And I play different keys

Ed Sheeran is talented
Ginger hair and plays guitar
Katy Perry acts and sings
She is beautiful and wears a hat.

Chloe Campbell (14)
Baston House School, Hayes

At 13

I wish 13-year-olds could drive
It would be a nice thing to aspire to
To be able to drive
Before 13, you could take exams
Then when you turned 13
You could then drive
And get a job
Grow up quickly.

Ianna Akarandut (12)
Baston House School, Hayes

Being Homeless

Being homeless is feeling hurt and hopeless.
Being homeless is being as hungry as a starving dog on the street.
Being homeless is feeling like you are a dirty tip.
Being homeless is being cold, freezing and desperate as an Arctic animal.
Being homeless is continuously wishing for a better, happier life.
Being homeless is being treated badly all the time like you're a trash can.

Riley (12)
Beaumont Leys School, Leicester

Down In The Deep

Down in the deep live many things
From small little fish to giant hungry sharks
As you go down the more you shall find
From creepy fish with no eyes to weird goblin sharks
Their mouths can move faster than a blink of an eye
You can go so deep that it's an alien world
Science says to live you need light
But mysterious plants find a way with nature's know-how
Things can live off the burning heat
Of the giant thermal vents that burn water over 100 degrees
Plastic and pollution ruin these seas
For whatever down there suffers more than me
The sea is great and should be protected
For whatever lives down in the deep
Is just as equal as those that breathe.

Hurshwen Nathan Chia (13)
Bickley Park School, Bickley

Baby Shark/An Old Man

Baby Shark
A baby shark called Little Ivor
Saw a deep-sea scuba diver.
He asked, "Mum, is that a manta ray?"
"No," she grinned, "that's a takeaway."

An Old Man
An old man took his phone to be fixed
The guy told him there was nothing wrong
The old man looked up in tears
And whispered, "So why don't my children ever call me?"

Laila Jennings (12)
Blenheim High School, Epsom

Make-Up And Malice

They hang around in cliques
Their voices bend your ears
It goes on for weeks
Months, years
They adjust their hair
Their cheeks, lips, eyes
They pollute the air
Their voices reaching new highs
Nobody tells them off
Even when they give lip
Nobody stops them
Nobody really let's rip
They make catty comments
Digging their claws in
Every cruel sentence
Making you feel like vermin
They face no consequences
They get in no trouble
They carry, carry on
Leaving you in the rubble
Make-up and malice
Knives in the lipstick
Poison in the blusher
Claws in the powder
Bullets in the lashes

They get away with it all
But they never leave a trace
They never leave a body
It's never anything physical
They're too sly for that
But they say it all
They're not below that
Subtle, they are
Never giving you a start
But every evil word
Pierces you through the heart
Every snarky saying
Is a fresh blemish
They show no scars
They powder over everything
While you remain ugly
A nobody, a nothing
Every cosmetic
Can hide their reality
Can doll them up
Give them new gravity
They're respected
Revered
Loved
The rest of us, though?
What of us rabble?
Us hoi-polloi?

We suffer
We live, just about
We die, painfully
Every single word
Killing
Us
Slowly
But they get away
They
Get
Away
With
It
All.

Marijela Obrenovic (15)
Bristnall Hall Academy, Oldbury

Mental Health

You're insecure about yourself,
You think bad about yourself but no one else.
No one knows what you go through,
You think they think you're fat and ugly too.

Your family thinks you are happy,
Really you feel floppy and snappy.
They'll say, "Oh, you'll be fine," but you're not.
You say to yourself, "It's for them not me."
You sit there and wonder to yourself, *why can't I be happy*
like everyone else?
"It's for attention"
"No need to cry"
You don't feel it, so why shouldn't I?
"It's fine you'll grow up with friends and wealth"
Maybe, but you don't realise it's affecting my mental health.

Tegan Shorney (12)
Brune Park Community School, Gosport

Sexism

In a world where women strive for success,
We're often met with sexism, which is a big fat mess.
We are underestimated and neglected by the men around us.

We are told to be pretty, to smile and nod, even in our saddest state.

When we are angry it's 'that time of the month'
But when a man feels the same, it's 'he's having a bad day'.
This is unfair, this sexism needs to stop!

We mustn't wear blue or green, that we stick to dolls and mustn't play with dinosaurs.

This is all too much! We are underrated and underpaid even in the 2020 decade!
We take so much hate, how are we ever meant to celebrate?
We are denied the jobs we want, our talents are overlooked and our voices ignored.
We feel like a needle in a haystack, a shadow, we feel alone.

This feels like a cage, a barrier to break.
It's like poison, so let's find the cure,
Not just for now but for the future.
Let's break the stereotypes and let our voices be heard.
Let's live in a world where gender doesn't define our fate.
Let's stop this sexism once and for all and make our world a better place.

Mabli Gruffudd-Pritchard (14)
Cardiff Montessori School, Llanishen

Home Sweet Home

The Earth is our home sweet home
But we've made it moan and groan
Air pollution, deforestation and climate change
Our actions have caused this harmful rage.

The oceans are full of plastic debris
Killing marine life without any plea
The ice caps are melting, oceans are rising
All this destruction, it's not surprising.

We need to act now and change our ways
Or we'll lose Earth in just a few days
Reduce, reuse and recycle more
Let's make the Earth green, like never before.

Plant more trees and save the rainforest
Let's pledge, to make Earth a better nest
Together we can make a difference
And save Mother Earth with our persistence

Let's not wait for tomorrow
And relieve Earth of its sorrow
Let's make steps, big and small
To heal and save Earth, once and for all.

Thomas Cassar (16)
Cottingham High School, Cottingham

Bullying

Why is it that when I talk you roll your eyes?
Why is it that when I sit down next to you
You smirk and roll your eyes?
Why is it you stop smiling
Around me and my friends?

What have we done wrong?

I am sure you know in yourself
Who you are and what you have done
Well, enough is enough.
I am done!
I am done trying to avoid you.
I am done trying to ignore you.
I don't need you in my life disrupting it, making it difficult.
You need to stop now!

Why is it you slam doors in our faces?
Why is it you laugh right in our faces?
Why is it you talk about us behind our backs
But try saying it to our face.
Oh that's right, you freeze.
All I have ever heard in my life is
'Freya, you will never do that'
'Freya, you are rubbish!'
But you are just another voice
Because I will achieve more than you

Seeing as bullying isn't a job, it's a choice
A choice you can make to either stand up and say it isn't
right
Or you can be the bully and one day regret your decision
And realise you made someone's day dark.
I cry myself to sleep at night
Just wishing it would stop
Maybe tomorrow it will cease
Then again, maybe not.

Freya Mason (11)
Cottingham High School, Cottingham

One Word

One word.
That's all it takes
To flood the entirety of someone's brain.
One word.
That's all it takes
To change a person's mindset for the next few days.
One word.
That's all you have to use.
Fat.
Ugly.
Short.
Nerd.
They may not seem like much but what they have in
common is that they are all one word.
That one word that cried someone to sleep.
That one word that came out of someone's mouth so
effortlessly yet travelled so deep.
So next time you want to say one word, don't.
Next time, think.
No matter if it only hurts them for a second, a day, a week.

Now you know why everything has changed about that
person you called fat, ugly, short or nerd.

Because of you,
And that one word.

Daisy Devereux (11)
Cottingham High School, Cottingham

A World That's Changing

The world is changing, it's what we fear,
As the consequences are faced each year,
The forests burn, the animals flee,
A world that's changing, can't you see?

Nature is a gift we should cherish,
From the mountains high and the seas that flourish,
The ice caps melt, the oceans rise,
A world that's changing before our eyes.

We must act now before it's too late,
Before our actions become our fate,
The oceans are warming, the coral reefs dying,
A world that's changing and we're not even trying.

Let's all work together, hand in hand,
To protect this world and our land,
The forests shrink, the animals disappearing,
A world that's changing and we're not even hearing.

Isabelle Fratson (13)
Cottingham High School, Cottingham

Two World Apocalypse

Now in darkness our world stops turning,
And now I hide,
Watching my home continue burning.

Now I sleep,
Trying to understand,
Why our world has to end.

Ashes now lie where the bodies were burning,
Now brainwashed our somewhat innocent minds,
Throwing my once clean eyes into a pit of fire
As the harmful bombs soar from higher.

It took two different worlds to start an apocalypse,
If only people ignored power.

What has our world come to?
If only we ignored those two.

Henry Sans Johnson (13)
Cottingham High School, Cottingham

Animal Abuse

Can you hear them crying?
Can you hear them screaming?
That's them left outside
All alone, nobody to love and care for them
Starving dogs, starving cats
Skinny as a newborn bat
Why buy a pet if you can't look after them?
Left out in the freezing cold
How would you feel?
Look after your pets, they have feelings too
Animal testing, that's also abuse
Stop all the neglect and hate
Stand up and help stop it
This can't carry on, it's horrific.

Cherry Austin (13)
Cottingham High School, Cottingham

Animal Cruelty

Animal cruelty...
I hate animal cruelty.
Small, big, medium,
They don't need to be abused.
Caged, tested, abandoned,
They are scared, frightened, terrified.
Zoos seem fine,
But most of their actual habitats are across the world.
Taken, forced out, kidnapped.
Families adopt pets just for them to be forgotten in a year.
Some families will abandon their pets when they get boring.

Reagan Jarvis-Shaw (13)
Cottingham High School, Cottingham

Kindness

Kindness is like a flower, a flower we can all plant,
And we can all give it to someone else,
In that case we are bees,
Spreading the pollen of kindness to help others grow.
The amazing thing about kindness
Is that although you might not want to be kind to a
particular person,
When you show random acts of kindness to them,
You just can't stop yourself from continuing.
Kindness makes us feel happy, and it makes others feel
happy too,
We start off as caterpillars, starting to be kind to others,
But soon enough the receiving and showing of constant
kindness
Morphs us into a butterfly, a kind person.

Caleb Tamale-Sali (12)
Cove School, Cove

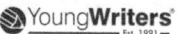
Let's Make Our World Smile

Hold up, take a minute and pause,
We need to talk about a really significant cause
We are suffocating our Earth,
With every problem that we birth,
And that *needs* to change
Problems - there's millions, there's thousands
Changing the world is a massive task,
But this is an issue we can't afford to mask
The ocean is full of pollution
And we *need* a solution
It doesn't matter your race or religion
This can never be a choice or decision
There is no Planet B
How can you not see?
Yes, we made mistakes in the past,
But these issues don't have to last
We are damaging our coral,
Do you really believe that this is moral?
Damaging creatures' homes,
Just for the government to pay off their loans.
As we need to all take the bait,
Because this ain't about love or hate,
What we do to our planet is our fate,

And we cannot be late,
To open that gate.
Of a different lifestyle.
Yeah, we may have to walk that mile,
But this is what we have to do to make our world smile.

Amy Cole (14)

Cromwell Community College, Chatteris

The World

Turtles are choking
Children are smoking
Poachers are hunting
Animal is being used as bunting
Polar bears are dying
People are sighing
And the world is slowly decaying.

Tilly Boniface (14)
Cromwell Community College, Chatteris

As They Go By

I sit in the window whilst they pass by
They laugh and they giggle
They smile and they cry
Behind all the glass
I'm not in the world
Curled in my blankets, thoughts of the world
And what's so bizarre
Is when I leave the door
I'm stuck with doubt
Thoughts tremble in
Comfort trembles out
Although I'm sure
I've never felt further away.

Erin Ramsey (12)
Danesfield CE School, Williton

I Want To Be Pretty

It's every day
Every day. I want to be pretty
It's always the same,
It always starts with water running down my eyes
And nails scratching my face
And I know some clothes don't fit me
And yes, I know I'm not as perfect as the other girls.

Every time I sit down, I need the oversized jacket.
I need the jacket to hide the ugliness.
I know what people think when people look at me.
Ugly, chubby, disgusting.
I just want to be like those girls.
Perfect, beautiful, pretty.
But no matter what. I can't. I want to be pretty.

I put the make-up on to hide the other beast.
I want to look like the princess the younger me wanted to be.
I want to be pretty.
I want to fit in clothes that are a size small,
I want to fit perfectly in my uniform,
I need to.
I don't want to start a waterfall down my face every day.

I want to save my tears for joy.
Not sadness.

I want to save my corset with fashion.
Not for curves.
I want to save my smile for happiness.
Not for disguise.
I want to be pretty.

Lexie Carvell (14)

Danetre And Southbrook Learning Village, Daventry

Earth Poem

With the greenest of trees and the healthiest planet in the solar system.
Earth is the best thing for our system.
All the animals enjoying life,
It surely couldn't get any better, right?
Well, yes, it can, but there is, and it's unfortunate to see this happen.
It's called climate change, where all the trees, leaves, icebergs and everything are going because of the monsters in this world.
Thankfully, this poem can help your needs to help the Earth, so let's do it.
First of all, animals are losing homes,
Like someone smashing glass domes.
Animals are losing food as all of it thrives in waters
So as animals start to die off, the Earth becomes duller.
But we can save it by recycling, not using fossil fuels and starting using solar energy instead,
Switching to an electric vehicle
Walk or bike so it doesn't pollute the air and use less hot water.
You know how to tackle climate change, so go out there and give climate change a taste of its medicine!

Jayden Rushton (12)
Danetre And Southbrook Learning Village, Daventry

About Love

Why do we love?
What is love?
Why do we do the things we do for people?

Love is what somebody does for you because they love you!

Like your mum, she cooks food for you because she loves
you!
Your dad drives you around because he loves you!
Your parents don't like cleaning your clothes, but they do it
so you don't smell.
They do it because they love you!

Your parents say don't go out with them today.
They say it so you don't get hurt or get in trouble.
They do it to protect you because they love you!

You love and they are always there for you.
They will still love you no matter what you do because that
is love!

Love can break and fix you!

But no matter what, you will always love that person.
You might get into silly little arguments.
But you'll still love them like I love my parents.
No matter what, they will always have a place in my heart.

Maggie-May Jalland-Baker (12)
Danetre And Southbrook Learning Village, Daventry

Creepy Robots

Trapped in an office alone
I sat and I sat...
Until I heard something coming...
Something was coming down the corridor.
I shut my door as fast as I could
I heard really loud banging coming from the door

I was waiting... waiting... and waiting
The banging finally stopped
I opened the door and started to explore
I saw animatronic-like robots on a stage
One rabbit holding a red guitar
One chicken with a cupcake in its hand
And one bear holding a microphone

There was one more robot that creeped me out
It was a fox with a hook as his right hand
I know it may not seem scary but trust me, it is
Suddenly I felt like something was talking to me in the
distance
The voice got closer... and closer...
I couldn't see where the voice was coming from
Suddenly I passed out...
I don't remember anything after that.

Fearne Badger (12)
Danetre And Southbrook Learning Village, Daventry

An Opportunity

You're called on; coldness introduces itself
As you're left in a shirt and trousers.
Stood in your lane, heart throbbing,
Fear of failure isn't helping.
The shot is heard and legs launch,
Within 8 seconds, you hear dings and it's over.
3rd is told, but something has changed.
You don't see failure, you see an opportunity for practise
And pushing yourself.
With this, who knows where you will place next time?

Xavier Deka (13)
Danetre And Southbrook Learning Village, Daventry

The Climb

I take a deep breath
before I start the climb,
I look up at certain death
will I make it up in time?

What lies at the top? Who knows
maybe clouds I suppose,
maybe it snows, maybe it glows
what lies at the top? Who knows

one last breath, and off I go
I go slow and cautious of what's below,
it's so low, like I was a while ago
although it would never show,

closer and closer to the top
I'm too close now I can't stop,
so much on my shoulders
I can so almost drop,

I've been going nonstop
finally I'm at the top,
I can drop everything
and finally, stop.

Henry Bendall (13)
Danetre And Southbrook Learning Village, Daventry

Missing You

What will happen when you die?
Can you fly? Would you cry?
Will you remember our last bye?
I'll always think of you when I look at the sky.

"I won't be here forever," you say,
That's why I've cherished every single day,
Until the day you passed away,
I cried every single day,

Will we ever meet again?
When would that time be? When?
You're in every thought of my mind
Even the moments when you were unkind

The pain in my heart feels like torture
And every night feels colder.
Every time I look at a beautiful view,
I always seem to be missing you.

Helen Loc (14)

Danetre And Southbrook Learning Village, Daventry

Her Heart

Whose heart is that? I think I know.
Its owner is quite sad, though.
It really is a tale of woe,
I watch her frown. I cry hello.

She gives her heart a shake,
And sobs until the tears make.
The only other sound's the break,
Of her wounded heart.

Her heart is big, broken and deep,
But she has promises to keep,
Until then, she shall not sleep.
So she lies in bed and weeps.

She rises from her bitter bed,
With thoughts of sadness in her head,
As she idolizes being dead.
Awaiting the day with never-ending dread.

Olivia Nawrocka (13)
Danetre And Southbrook Learning Village, Daventry

Against All Odds

In 2023, from top to bottom
against all odds
Notts County bottom of the League
just waiting for success, they did it
winning game after game
new signings and more money, finally feeling good
back to their old selves and then FA Cup time
Notts County vs Wrexham
3-2 loss, all hope was lost
but then a chance at winning the playoffs
game after game, win after win
and then the final - Notts were going to Wembley
all pressure and hopes were high
we did it.
The Magpies won the playoffs.

Mason Baker (14)
Danetre And Southbrook Learning Village, Daventry

Very Metal!

I listen to music of motivation
Thrash metal in my ear
Bitter words of anarchy
I hold the lyrics near

I am who I am
Your harassment does not change me
I will be me
Cut my hair
Make you stare
Until you sneer
Because your disgusted gasp
Pumps me with raging passion

I raise a fist of protest
My battle jacket in hand
I stomp on the opinions of fascists
Whilst rocking to my favourite band.

Evie Jones (13)
Danetre And Southbrook Learning Village, Daventry

We Need To Make A Change

Summers are getting hotter,
Faced with spells of drought.
Our climate is now changing,
It's true without a doubt.

The Earth is your home, yet you destroy,
Its skin and bone.
The Earth needs love,
And the Earth needs care,
Because you are polluting its air.

The Earth is where we live,
And it's our only one.
The damage that has been made,
Needs to come undone.

Elianna Wojnicki (11)
Danetre And Southbrook Learning Village, Daventry

I Don't Know What To Write

I don't know what to write.
It is so hard to think,
It's like I am stuck
I don't know what to write.

All my feelings overwhelmed,
Don't know what to do
I am stuck, not knowing what to do.

Word after word, not knowing.
I don't know what to write.
Here comes someone to help
Now I know what to do
It's so much fun now
I know what to do.

Alisha Barber (12)
Danetre And Southbrook Learning Village, Daventry

Daventry Town FC

Daventry Town have dominated the league
Getting to a cup final as well vs Parkland Tigers!
An unbeaten team
Who beat Dav 3-1 a couple games before.
Scoring two lucky goals,
The last ten minutes.

But the question is...
Can Dav beat Parkland Tigers?

Yes, they can!

Daventry Town thrash Parkland out of the park.
4-1 to Daventry Town.

Joseph Howells (11)
Danetre And Southbrook Learning Village, Daventry

Gorilla Tag

We are swinging, we are branching.
Lava monkeys chasing.
Running for life.
Oculus dying - needs recharging.
Sweats be sweating.
Controllers be breaking.
Creators be filming.
Modders be modding.
Minigames be getting played.
People getting banned.
Only g tag players will,
Understand the struggle
To not hit the TV while playing Gorilla Tag.

Giulia Cirja (12)
Danetre And Southbrook Learning Village, Daventry

Brayden

When you fight him you will feel fright
He will knock you out and say goodnight
His boxing skills are equal to pros
If you fight him he will break your nose
In the ring he will be crowned king
He is made of steel in the fight
He will make you squeal
Don't mess with him. He will make you kneel
He might have nits, but he will land a few hits.

Ethan Williams-Marsh (13)

Danetre And Southbrook Learning Village, Daventry

Lost At Sea

Lost at sea
Where can I go?
Is there an island nearby - I don't know.
I'm so hungry I'm going to starve
I have some bread but only half
Waves are rising, I better be quick,
The boat keeps shaking, I'm gonna be sick
I wake up on shore with a sigh of relief
But only to realise I'm beyond the reef.

Jack Retief (12)
Danetre And Southbrook Learning Village, Daventry

The Final

They feel the pressure,
It's getting closer,
They are ready in the luxury leisure,
Can they win?
It will be very thin,
They come out on the pitch,
The referee blows the whistle,
It's time to start the clock,
It goes *tick-tock*,
Will they flop
Or will they come out on top?

Cyran Davies (12)
Danetre And Southbrook Learning Village, Daventry

Pollution

Rubbish fills the streets,
and toxins fill the air
we're destroying the planet and it's not fair.

Trees are dying,
animals too
if we don't clean up, we will too!

Earth getting warm,
ice is melting
so we should really, really start helping.

Jacob Hines (12)
Danetre And Southbrook Learning Village, Daventry

Nothing Left To Lose

I don't know what to do
To get me back to you.
I've got nothing left to lose
I'm sadness, tears and blues.
All bridges have been crossed
I guess our love is lost.
I've got no more tears to cry
So here's one last goodbye.

Leilani Albert (12)
Danetre And Southbrook Learning Village, Daventry

Pollution

Pollution fills the air.
People are in the streets,
In cars driving.
Did you need to drive when you could have walked?
This makes it worse.
The breathing gets hard.
So stop polluting our streets.

Charlie Cullinane (12)
Danetre And Southbrook Learning Village, Daventry

Times Have Changed

Generations have changed, people are mocking each other.
Lots of people think harassment is okay. Because it is
natural.
Old generations are mocking the people now who are
concerned for the planet.
'Boys will be boys' is what they say.
I say that it's pathetic, girls can't do the same and get told
off.
People say 'respect your elders' when it's not given, it's
earned.
Lots of people say 'they're just going through a phase and
saying they're gay just for attention... they just haven't
found the right person yet'.

Warning people the world is ending is fake, it is a real thing.
Scientists from NASA are getting arrested for protesting.
Amanda Gorman is inspiring me to tell people it's unfair.
Really, should a 12-year-old have to do this just to warn
people of their own mistakes?
No! Is a full sentence like a 'you' tell someone to stop.
It makes me angry that the old people are not forgiving us
for messing up the planet.
No one is sad for the animals that are extinct.
Gone... This is my warning for everyone who is being bullied,
sad for the animals and trying to help.

Mia Holt-Barker (13)
Ecclesfield School, Sheffield

Cruelty To One Another

Prejudice, discrimination, do you know how it affects people?
People try to make themselves feel bigger by making others feel smaller.
This has to stop, otherwise, it will not only make people feel depressed,
But it will affect their grades, their social life and who they grow to be.
This cannot carry on.

If you think, have you ever said something that you didn't think was prejudiced or discriminative, but to that person, it is?
And you didn't think before you spoke.
Then a friendship you could have had,
You subconsciously threw it away.
And, the worst part is, you can't take it back,
You have to live with that.
So it is not only damaging to the target, but also to the speaker.

We can discriminate against someone online, face-to-face,
Physically or mentally,
But we shouldn't be doing any at all, should we?
Think before you speak.
I have been told that my entire life.

Now I will tell you
Think, don't just do.
Do what is right, don't be discriminative or prejudiced.

Kira Green (11)
Ecclesfield School, Sheffield

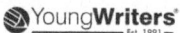

Change In Our World

Let's change the world and fix it
Shift it and lift it, remake it and shape it
Fly where there is hope, where it's green
Where the air and water is clean.

Let's fix what's broken
And brave the unspoken
Let's rise and say how we've changed the world today
What we want is never simple but we can achieve it

We need another chance to fix our mistakes
We need to be forgiving and kind
The world needs us to be better humans
We can do it, we can do it, just believe.

Ebony Hanson (13)
Ecclesfield School, Sheffield

Kindness

K indness is for everyone,
I n the world,
N ot everyone gets it.
D on't be rude, you don't know others' backstories.
N ot everyone's life is amazing,
E ven if it seems like it,
S o you have to give kindness,
S tarting from today.

Kindness is for you.

Phoebe Clayton
Ecclesfield School, Sheffield

Environment

Trees help us to breathe
Without them we would grieve
We need to stop cutting them down
They're looking at us with a frown

Animals' habitats are being destroyed
The animals are really quite annoyed
Without animals the world would be quite dull
But the zoos are quite full.

Elina Pym (11)
Ecclesfield School, Sheffield

Love Who You Are

6am, when he wakes up, he wipes the sleep from his eyes.
Another day at school again weighing heavy upon his mind.
Standing tall, trying to keep it cool; saying yes to everything.
He's lost in doubt, all he cares about is finding a way of
fitting in.
Don't ever forget to love, keep loving who you are.
Don't ever forget to shine, shining like a star.
There's something so perfect, courage in everyone,
So don't ever let yourself stop loving who you are.

She stood by her mirror; wondering how to fix her scarf.
Filled with fear of people staring from afar.
At the way she talks, just how she walks.
It's tearing up her self-esteem, she's lost in doubt,
All she cares about is finding a way of fitting in.

Rayan Ali (12)
Eden Boys Leadership Academy East, Birmingham

Conflict Within Me

The brain over this, it is,
It has lost the fight.
Leave the world, it desires.
As hope slowly fades.

Bleeding, it is always.
Betrayed by someone new
Betrayed by the trusted, which are very few.
However, present it still is,
As the heart remains a friend of his.

It is able to forgive, so live long it may.
The past is now a memory that behind will stretch far away.

Mohamed El Bikry (14)
Eden Boys Leadership Academy East, Birmingham

A Winter Wonderland

A winter wonderland is magical, cold and snowy.
Freezing snowflakes, try to catch them on your tongue.

A winter wonderland is fun. Snowball fights,
Snowmen, falling off your sledge, losing your wellies.

A winter wonderland is pretty when the Northern Lights
come out,
Reds and yellows, orange and pink,
Blues and turquoise, teal and green.
Come out and have a look.

A winter wonderland is exciting, all your family home who
you haven't seen in ages.
The smell of the tree, games around the table before you go
to bed.
The presents left by Santa.

A winter wonderland is freezing, makes you tired and
exhausted from all the hard work.
Hot chocolate and marshmallows make you warm in your
stomach.
A feast in a mug!

Tired, exhausted and happy.
A very good day.

Kealan Mackenzie (14)
Gairloch High School, Gairloch

I See You

One of the things I have always feared,
maybe so much I admired, about this world -
and the people in it - is the hold
that this society has on each other.
The capability we have on how a person
reflects and views themselves.
We cause each other sadness and
self-consciousness and hate,
or we cause happiness and
self-confidence and love.

Which is the way he makes me feel.
He makes me feel like I could be in a room
with millions of gorgeous girls,
who would be valued by anyone's eyes
to be a lot more attractive than I am,
but he makes sure I always know
in every circumstance
that he only wants me and only has romantic
love for me.

And I know how that boy feels
about himself,
how he hates the way he acts
and the way he looks.
I know he hates himself and

criticises himself and believes his worth
is simply nowhere near as good as mine is.
All because of society and the people that surround him.
But to me his worth seems more than mine.
And I don't care if one day it kills me,
I want to spend every day of this
god-forsaken life,
in this messed-up world making him recognise his worth
like I do.
Honestly, the way I feel about this boy
and the things I would do to prove it to him,
I would die for him.
I love him.

But you shouldn't need someone else
to make you feel like this,
to feel valued and beautiful and confident.
We shouldn't have to fear society
and their words,
fear going outside because of what people say,
no matter what we look like,
how much we weigh, how our body looks,
or our race. We should
all
be
valued.

Aine Martin (15)

Golspie High School, Golspie

Swimming In The Future

The ocean,
With its woken waves,
Sparkly shells
And the sand,
Sand as soft as icing sugar
Luxurious as can be.
Sat by the beach
Our clean beaches,
With nothing but sand, tourists
Smelling of freshly squeezed sunscreen.
But this is the past
Not the present
Today I visit the ocean,
Thinking of what it was
Before the treacherous ways of our society
How people mindlessly destroy our beaches,
Along with our planet
And why?
For what reasons?
Fast food and disposability.
Why do we make the sealife suffer
Because of your litter
Plastic bottles,
Straws, plastic bags
Cigarette butts

And sickly sweet wrappers
Why don't we change?
Our selfish ways
So the sealife can live
The way they have for centuries
Before man arrived
Why can't we save innocent creatures
Why can't we think
Think of the fish being suffocated
And intoxicated by us
By the way we live and
What we do

Which simply cannot continue.

Lexie Macleod (14)

Golspie High School, Golspie

Red Light

The bitter cold was like a slap to the face, shocking
Tall trees caked in a thick layer of frost
Icy roads

Brace yourself
Raindrops like bullets suddenly firing down at us
There wasn't a chance, never another opportunity

The silence said it all
Yet hope still latched onto me like a loose thread

Then a traffic light in the distance

The colour crimson shone brightly
Illuminating us
I saw red

And doubt in the windows to his soul, tears too
He said he would never cry, he said he was tough
But susceptibility was making him tremble

He was in front of me within milliseconds
Open arms; a needy invitation
It happened inevitably

His strong arms wrapped forcefully around me
Like a snake slithering around its prey

I was engulfed by him

No way would I ever leave
No way would I ever escape.

Alisha Lone (14)
Hall Green School, Hall Green

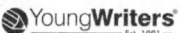
The Voice Of Anxiety

I wrote it down as I can't say,
From the outside I seem okay.
I stand while they laugh and play,
The voice inside me says it's not okay.
Look at her so petite and pretty,
Why don't I look like that? What a pity.

As tears roll down my cheeks,
I get the message, meet me here,
They're everywhere,
So I go to get ready.
As per usual I overthink,
My brain is full of cloud and mist.
Help me find the medication,
Help me find the cure,
I can't seem to think without it so help me find some more.
I can't go here, I can't go there,
Without the little voice in my mind.

Chelsie Quinn (12)
Horizon Community College, Barnsley

The Long Way Home

Blue sky like the ocean and the big green field,
Where beautiful flowers of different colours adorned that field,
The old tree was reflected in the crystalline lake
Where some birds rest.

The cold of the night hugged me,
As the big full moon followed me
Along the long way home,
And the stars shone like diamonds in the sky.

Andreea Nita (13)
Horizon Community College, Barnsley

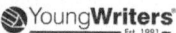
Video Games

Why?
Why do we play?
Why not be active?
Why?
Video games are good,
Video games are bad,
It's your decision to make.
Why do we play all day?
Why don't we touch the grass?
Why?
Games make you angry,
Games make you sad
But they make you glad.
We have different actions,
We have different minds,
But we have the same quality of games.
We are so different
But we do the same with video games.

Ibrahim Yusuf (12)
Hornchurch High School, Hornchurch

Stop Deforestation

Habitats being destroyed,
Animals being killed,
Why must we do this to get materials?
This is life, this is unfair.

We get to live,
We get to grow,
They get nothing but no home.

We can change,
We can fix this,
This doesn't hurt us,
But it hurts them.

Animals should grow,
Animals should live,
Why did they deserve this?

Sydney Allsopp (11)
Hornchurch High School, Hornchurch

Sleep

Sleep, however hard insomnia tries,
Will always be enjoyable.

Sleep, however hard insomnia tries
Will always be a necessity.

Sleep, however hard insomnia tries
Will always happen eventually.

Sleep, however hard insomnia tries
Will always find you.

Sleep, however hard insomnia tries
Will always be there for you.

Teddy Scott (14)
Hornchurch High School, Hornchurch

Guns

I thought guns were cool...
I mean, I haven't used one,
But I just thought they looked cool.
I have a few Nerf guns...
I got a Nerf gun for my birthday,
But I don't know what made me want it.
I play this game called Fortnite,
It's a bit like a modern warfare game, but with no blood.
I got the game on the 26th of April 2022.
I loved it... but none of the girls did.
Maybe it was just a boy thing...
I don't know.
I think it's weird that you are allowed
To have guns in America but not in England...
I wonder why?

Ned Rowcroft (12)

Macmillan Academy, Middlesbrough

I Won't Stay Silent

Silenced and ignored, my voice fades away
But I won't let them silence me, not today
I'll speak up and shout, let my words ring out
Until they hear me without a doubt

As I raise my voice, my power grows
And my message spreads like a rose
I won't be silenced, I won't be ignored
My voice is strong and I won't be bored

So let's raise our voices and make them heard
Until the world listens to every word.

Cobie-Sharon Harrison (12)
Macmillan Academy, Middlesbrough

Dear Brother Or Sister

Dear brother or sister,
We have to stand together to fight the unfairness,
That your son or your daughter will face,
When there is no food or clean water,
Because of our paper,
We need to say see you later to the paper,
And be a planter of new trees,
So that my brother and sister can live.
Do you want the future generations to live,
Or do you want them to have to worry,
About all our water and paper?

Anna Pearson (12)
Macmillan Academy, Middlesbrough

I Am Dying

Listen to me... I am dying.
See me... I am changing.
Hear me... I am in pain.

My water is polluted by your toxic greed.
My air is intoxicated by your selfishness.
My animals are suffering at your hands.

How would you feel if you were me?
How would you survive without me?

Think before you act.
Think before it's too late.

Listen to me... I am dying.

Omar Elmorsy (13)
Macmillan Academy, Middlesbrough

No More Litter!

Litter is an unknown crime,
And we are running out of time,
As if we are stuck in a hole,
And can't get out.
We need a helping hand,
To save our land!
This is no joke, this is no drill.
It's the reality,
And I need you to agree.
To save our planet,
And save ourselves.

Lily Duffy (12)
Macmillan Academy, Middlesbrough

Nature's Beauty

The lush, emerald carpet of grass coated the landscape,
Imposing mountains which looked like grey daggers stood in
the distance,
Towering trees swayed back and forth as the wind danced
round them
and the river, a twisting and turning blanket of blue,
stretched out its body through the haven of beauty and
nature.
The sun's one golden and malevolent eye gazed down on
the ground below,
Majestic birds glided around the woodland, leaving a trail of
colour and joy wherever they went
Great houses, that were built out of the finest materials
known to man, sat on the blanket of green
And each one was filled with the sound of children's
laughter.
The tranquillity of nature surged through the earth's floor
and life began to grow,
Marigold flowers dotted the landscape as new ones began
to explode into wonderlands of colour,
Twisting and turning roots climbed up the bark of the trees
as if they were a shield trying to protect it,
Everything was perfect, it was as if it had been beautifully
designed and forged, perhaps by God.

Zain Ahmed (12)
Manchester Grammar School, Fallowfield

Draughts

The game of draughts is like an argument
Everyone sets out to win
You start off with small steps
Moving diagonal across the board
Trying to dodge your opponent
But they strike you by surprise
And knock you down
Again and again
As they start beating you, but slowly you start fighting back
And the great chase starts, you move then they move
Until you corner your opponent
Then you strike your final move
And you eventually win.

Grace Wilkinson (13)
Netherthorpe School, Staveley

Fallen War Heroes

We are soldiers
Strong and brave
Fighting for our family
And our lives

We are soldiers
Fallen war soldiers
Forgotten over time

We are soldiers
We are true
Here for your every need
We are loyal servants in
A cruel, cruel world
Trying to keep the balance
And peace

We are soldiers
Shunned away from society
At last, our pain
Is free

We are soldiers
Of the dead
Drowned of all our glee
Now, we shall be free
Of all the pain.

Our sacrifice
We have received

To let go
Of hope and
Be buried
Where we live eternally

Where we
Get flashbacks
Of our
Last days and the one fatal bullet
Piercing us and our memories of our youth

Our wives and
Children mourning our
Deaths, waiting for us to
Come through the door as
They drowned their face, not believing
The truth, later to move and forget.

Corey Cifaldi-Wyatt (12)

New College Leicester, Leicester

These Clothes

These clothes were designed to look cool
To look stylish
To look trendy

These clothes were designed to be accessible
To meet consumers' demand
To be cheap

These clothes were designed for one wear
To create micro trends
To end up in landfill

These clothes were designed to be thrown in rivers
To release their toxic dyes
Killing animals

These clothes were designed to be made
Without pay
And twenty-four-hour working days

These clothes were designed to destroy the planet
To make rich owners richer
To pay workers less than a living wage

These clothes need to stop
Stop being bought
Stop being made.

Primrose Morrall (15)
Sands School, Ashburton

Do You Honestly Not Care?

When you look through the bars of the cage,
Do you honestly not feel any rage?
When you cook what you eat,
Do you not think about the cows and the sheep,
That died for that piece of meat?
Do you honestly not care,
For the bear,
That died for that rug,
Or do you just sit there all smug?
Do you honestly think that's fair,
When you buy products for your hair?
Do you check whether it's ethical,
So nothing is injected with some chemical?
Do you honestly not feel any guilt,
For the animals whose blood is spilt?

Maggie Morrall (15)
Sands School, Ashburton

Busy World

A man in a suit sits worrying,
A stream gently flows over smooth rocks,
A breeze gently shifts the green of the trees.

A man sits worrying,
While a golden light shines through the clouds,
And the birds sing.

A man sits surrounded by the undisturbed flowers and reeds,
Listening to the sounds of the Earth.

A man sits in peace,
Watching a mountain break through the glowing mist above,
Thoughts let go.

Jasper Wake
Sands School, Ashburton

Don't Throw Away Your Life!

Don't throw away your life,
underestimating the effects of drugs could leave you
addicted, poor and alone.
Drugs don't fix things, they are not a coping mechanism,
they are not a friend you can turn to when going through
life struggles.
Speak to a person, not the hallucinated confusion your mind
created due to the effects of drugs.
They might sound fun, exciting, but no,
even the slightest consumption could lead to life-
threatening consequences.
Life over, money gone, no friends, miserable life, pure
depression.
Ditch drugs, research rehabilitation, road to recovery, fix
your feelings.
Don't throw away your life.

Phoebe Hardy (12)

Sir Robert Pattinson Academy, North Hykeham

Does That Make You Happy?

I am gone
Taken
My life
Destroyed
My mind
Broken
You win.
Happy?

I fought
Never knowing why you attacked
I lived
Knowing I would die
I loved
Knowing I would never be accepted
I lost
Knowing I would lose
Glad?

I never pleased you
Never good enough
Again I ask
Are you happy now?

My life is in ruins
Are you pleased?

I remember
Every
Word
Action
Feeling
And I will never forget.
Are you content?

It was me against an army
I am dead
In my mind.

Does that make you happy?

Sophia Arbuthnot (12)
St George's School, Harpenden

Pain

Sitting in the classroom
Asking to go to the bathroom
Sitting at home
On your phone
Both different
But not that different
Especially not in your brain
It's all the same pain
Sitting on a field
That field as your shield
Cupboards you raid
Trying to find a blade
Things get hard
But don't put up that guard
It's all mental health
Don't blame yourself.

Lexi Smart (15)
St Margaret Ward Catholic Academy, Tunstall

Power Of War In Ukraine

In Ukraine, a war rages on,
A conflict that seems never gone,
With power struggles at its core,
And lives lost by the score.

Brothers once, now torn apart,
Fighting for different hearts,
With guns and bombs and tanks so loud,
The cries of pain rise from the ground.

In cities once so full of life
Now rubble left to tell the strife,
Families fleeing, seeking peace,
Hoping for all the fighting to cease.

The power of war is a fearsome thing,
Tearing apart what was once a dream,
Destroying homes, hopes, and hearts
Leaving behind only broken parts.

But still, there are those who believe,
That a brighter future they can achieve,
Where peace reigns over the land,
And love unites all hand in hand.

May that day soon come to pass,
And the power of war be a thing of the past,

Where Ukraine can once again be whole,
And love and peace can reign forevermore.

Tinisha Watt (12)

St Roch's Secondary School, Glasgow

A Wound That Never Heals

A curse that haunts us from our birth,
Sexism, a plague that stains the earth,
A cancer that spread, a poison that kills,
A blight that shatters hearts and wills.

From the workplace to the home,
It robs us of our rights and tone,
An unequal world, a biased fate,
A reality that we can't debate.

Women, the victims of this vice,
Stripped of their power, robbed of their prize
Judged by their gender, denied their worth
Their potential trapped, their dreams unearthed.

But sexism hurts us all the same,
Men too, trapped in its narrow frame,
Expected to conform, to be macho and strong,
To hide their fears, to never go wrong.

We need to break free from this chain,
To see each other as equals again,
To cherish diversity, to embrace the whole,
To build a world that honours every soul.

Sexism, a curse we must fight,
To create a future that's just and bright,
Where every voice is heard, every talent blooms,
And we can all dance to life's vibrant tunes.

Amber (12)

St Roch's Secondary School, Glasgow

Scottish Weather

A haiku

Scottish weather is
Mostly raining and soaking
So, wear a jacket.

Connor Wallace (14)
Stirling High School, Stirling

Please Can People Lower Their Expectations?

Please can people lower their expectations
Before we affect our future generations?
With this constant fear of not fitting in
Yet we are still expected to keep up a grin

We are holding everything in, holding it close
To our longing chests so nobody knows
Because what if people ever found out?
What would they then think about?

Would they see us in a different light?
Would they see that our lives are just fight after fight?
Would they make a rude, dismissive comment?
Would we have to listen to their righteous judgement?

We feel like we are meant to be perfect constantly
That's why it's not a surprise that we are fading away
instantly
This world is horribly lonely to us
We are invisible until we step out of line or cuss

This is why we smile and fake it
We will never surrender, never admit
How tired, drained and alone we feel
Because, to anyone else, it's not a big deal

Our generation has got it tough
And I'm not surprised when people say they've had enough
Every day is a constant battle
To prove our worth, makes us rattle

We have been brainwashed into keeping our issues to
ourselves
When, in reality, people struggle day after day to keep
floating themselves
People my age consider themselves as a burden
Sometimes just because of one specific person

It goes unseen when we pass expectations
So, we are still yet to hear the word 'congratulations'
Instead, we have to live with this never-ending
misinterpretation
That all we do is cause riots and this situation

I don't think people truly understand how drastic this issue
has become
This worldwide problem is often classed as invalid or dumb
When, in reality, there are people dying
And feel like they have to give up trying

Does it make people feel good, making innocent people like
us feel bad?
Please can people lower their expectations?

Isla Speirs (14)
Stirling High School, Stirling

Differences

What are differences?
Why differences?
Our differences are a gift from God to distinguish us from
people and races.
So, let's treat it right,
And use it right.
We might be different in the colour of our skin,
to the languages we speak,
to the way we speak, and how we speak,
to the beliefs we practice,
Or the cultures or background we come from
But we have the same colour blood.
Differences will always exist because
our differences are often a healthy sign of good progress
that should not always lead to a rift or division between us.
In life you can make progress by accepting and using your
difference,
or making excuses by putting yourself down and not being
you.
Our differences are like walls
barricading us from our true unique selves
so let's use our difference to be unique and offer something
that no one else can offer to the world.
So, I say,

Be different.
Be you.
Be unique and progress in life.

Keon Odulawa
Stone Lodge School, Dartford

War

They stamp their feet
Move to the beat
Never see life
When all you see is defeat

The power they hold
The winner has been sold
The winner has been seen
That winner is me

They stamp and shout
Mess about
The war is out
The war is about
They clash their swords
And ask their lord,
"Do we have permission to kill?"
"Do we have will?"

They march in time
Shouting in line
Throwing their spears
We will be fine?

They are coming,
The war is humming
The war has just begun.

Krystal Proctor (12)
The Axholme Academy, Crowle

Victory Is Ours

I pull up my socks and tie up my laces,
Ready to travel to all the places.
On tour with my new team,
So excited I could scream.

Here we go on the road.
Just a bit more time
Let's go.

We're here now ready to play,
I feel nervous but I can do it
Captain my team out on the field

I pass the ball to number 12
Then kicks it to me and I receive
I take the shot and we succeed

We score!
And the crowd starts to roar

It's been 45 minutes and it's half time
We're 1-nil up and not much time
Keep the score and victory will be ours.

Eliza Thurbon (11)
The Chauncy School, Ware

Tranquillity

Fear crawled towards me as I ambled through this dense forestation,
An ominous glow stalked my every move,
Frantically my eyes scanned the bushes for life,
Soft rustling sounds flooded my ears;
I was trekking through this wonderland.
I turned and soft, fluffy feathers deceived this part of the land.
What part of the land is this? I approached -
Help me!
Vultures circled me as birds of prey found their food...

Korey Lovatt (12)
The Hart School, Rugeley

Money, Money, Money

Money comes,
Money goes. Where does it go?
Goodness knows.
Money is a valuable thing...
But why is it so precious?
Without money you're considered poor
And with it you're considered wealthy.
People get crazy over money and would do anything for money!
I mean everyone wants to be rich, besides,
I'm not taking sides.
For the love of money,
We would sell our very souls away.

Iqra Karim (14)
The Hyndburn Academy, Rishton

In This Situation...

Anything. Anything can be used against you
Your height, your weight, your music taste
Your name, your voice, the career of your choice
The way you walk, the way you act
Whether you have a dog or a cat
There is nowhere you can go and nothing you can do
Without having someone somewhere say something to you
You could be at school with your friends
When a teacher asks to see you when school ends
You were framed for something you didn't do
But in this situation, who can save you?
On your way back from school all alone
One of your bullies follows you home
They make comments and shout things at you
But in this situation, who can save you?
With your 'friend' on a call
They laugh and tease because you fall
Deep inside it really hurts you
But in this situation, what can you do?
Being yourself and people look at you weird
Pointing you can see and whispers you can hear
You know they're talking about you
But in this situation what can you do?
Nothing you can do, nothing you can say
To make these painful comments stop and go away

Comments on your hair or what you wear
Comments on your face or your walking pace
Someone will always have something to say
But you need to remember not to shy away
You'll always have people that trust you
You need to remember to trust them too.

Eva Vasiliauskaite (13)
The Hyndburn Academy, Rishton

The Pain Of War

In a daze, a fog in mind,
Trembling with fear, how will I cope?
Remembering what I have left behind,
Searching in the deadly night for some hope,
The sound of bullets, piercing my soul,
Only knowing there is one way to go,
Anything to get us out of this dirty death hole,
knowing that there are still many shells yet to blow,
I keep on gaining more unimaginable pain,
When will things finally be peaceful again?

Toni Elsworthy (13)
The Market Weighton School, Market Weighton

Under The Surface

I look happy 'cause I'm joking around,
but under the surface I'm crying on the ground,
I want to go home, not be stuck in this little zone,
the only thing I've got to take my mind off reality is my
phone.
The rules are so strict, they are making me sick,
I feel I have no say because I'm a kid, stop taking the mick.
On-site at school, don't get to meet anyone new,
teachers and staff are nice, but I still feel blue,
nothing makes a difference in my mind,
even when people try to be kind.
Yes, that's me larking around, people see me happy,
but I'm still lying on the ground!

Daisy Tyrer (15)
The Meadows School, Dove Holes

Race 1, Race 2, Race All For You

In memory of Hill Sixteen, Envoye Special and Dark Raven

If I break my leg, I get a bullet to the head,
Running this race unaware of our fate,
All for the money, that goes to those men,
The slightest mistake, the faster the pace,
The faster the pace, the riskier the stakes,
The sound of the hooves beating the ground
As deafening screams erupt from the crowd,
Our jockeys make us go through very tight spaces
Unbeknown of what we may face when we up the pace
Not all of us make the finishing line
But the ones that do will continue to wonder
When will it be their time...

Grand National 2023

Caitlin Portsmouth (15)
The Meadows School, Dove Holes

Don't Forget Me

Don't forget me, though I am burrowed away,
You may never find me but you must try,
Through the rubble-filled streets and smoky sky,
I'm like a golden beacon in a black-and-white world.

I remember when I shone and swirled,
And children's laughter filled the air,
As I shone, brighter than the fear,
But then, like the sun on a winter's day,
The clouds came and I went away.

But still I am here though you may not see me,
A faint memory at the back of your mind,
On the tip of your tongue as you try to unwind,
The web of lies you create,
As your world fills with untruths and hate.

So remember me, that four-letter word,
That signifies so much more than it's worth,
I am with you always, though you may think you've lost me.
For I am hope.

Marla Babiker (12)
The Oratory Preparatory School, Goring Heath

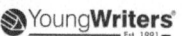
Be Bold, Be You

Amidst a world of prejudice and scorn,
Where people are judged before they're born,
There stands a cry for equality,
Of gender and skin colour, with no partiality.

For centuries, women have been confined,
To the kitchen and the role of kind,
Their talents obscured, their minds constrained,
A life of servitude restrained.

But the world is slowly waking up,
To the power of a woman, her spirit and her guts,
She can lead, she can govern, she can invent,
All she needs is a chance to prove her mettle, and she
won't relent.

In the same vein, skin colour too,
Has been the subject of hateful views,
Black people have been the target of discrimination,
For years, despite being a part of any given nation.

It is high time we embrace,
Our fellow humans of every race,
Discriminating them based on colour or gender,
Is a curse upon humanity, we must always remember.

For each of us has the same dreams,
The same aspirations, the same screams,

And it is only by treating each other as equals,
Can we build a world, with no division or sequels.

So let us celebrate our diversity,
And denounce any form of adversity,
Let us build a world where love conquers hate,
And where equality for all is the ultimate fate.

Ozzie Visser (12)
The Oratory Preparatory School, Goring Heath

Make It Stop

W ar is tactical
A rmies are stronger than ever
R emorse is something no one sees,

I f you let war carry on, then who are you?
N ever let a person die if you can stop it

U ntil you know you have done all you should, you should never stop
K illing can be stopped, we just have to unite
R ise up and stop war together
A lthough you shouldn't do that with your fist
I nstead use your most powerful weapon
N ever doubt it and always use it, your voice
E verything would be peaceful then.

Asher Gray (12)

The Oratory Preparatory School, Goring Heath

Pandemic

The pandemic hit us hard and fast,
Our lives were changed, our plans were dashed.
We turned to social media to stay connected,
And found a new way to stay protected.

Online we chatted, laughed and cried,
Shared our stories and deep inside,
We found a way to stay together,
Even when we were apart forever.

Social media was a lifeline,
A way to stay connected all the time.
It helped us through the darkest days,
And brought us closer in so many ways.

Beth Crate (14)
Tomlinscote School, Frimley

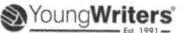

Together

In the lands, far and wide
Where the sun beats down with pride
There are those who must go hungry
Making their stomachs rumble loudly

World hunger is a problem so vast
It affects millions with its grasp
From Africa to Asia and beyond
It is a battle that's ongoing, on and on

For some, food is normal and dear
While for others, it is just a mere
A luxury we can easily afford
A bounty we take for granted and hoard

But for those who must go without
Their struggle is something we cannot doubt
Their bellies empty, their spirits low
Struggling to find a way to grow

The causes of hunger, there are many
From poverty to war, it is plenty
But whatever the reason may it be
We must work together, you and me

To end this tragedy once and for all
To give hope to those who may feel small

We must fight with all our might
To make sure everyone has a bite

So, let's join and let's make a start
Let's do our bit with a kind heart
For a world without hunger sounds like a dream
That's within our reach, or so it seems...

Liam Dickinson (12)
Wellingborough School, Wellingborough

Ban The Liv Tour

The Liv tour is crushing the golf competition
Golf is becoming a sport of money
It does not feel the same anymore
The PGA is the true tour of golf
Sport isn't an investment
Dustin Johnson, Brooks Koepka
Bryson Dechambeau
They're not leaving for pride
They're leaving for money
We are on the fairway
No need to hit it to the bunker
Please bring golf together again.

Harrison Gillard (12)
Wellingborough School, Wellingborough

Stop The Wars Around The World

Wars are destroying the world
Poor people begging to survive
Gunfire in the air fire flares are in the lairs
Explosions and missiles fear the cheerful
Loads of people die because of gunfire
Big bad bombs destroy by the hour.

Henry Summerfield (12)
Wellingborough School, Wellingborough

I'll Try

You may mock and judge me for the way I spell,
For my illegible handwriting
But, still I try

My loudness may annoy you
But my voice is my mask
I go louder to feign confidence
But, don't let it deceive you

As with the certainty of life, death and taxes,
I'll fake it till I make it
No matter what, you can't take it away
And still I try

Do you want to see me fail?
To rip up my work and throw it in the bin
See me crying with frustration, at the injustice of it all
Knowing how hard it is for me to win

Does my standing up for myself offend you?
You take it as if it's personal
I'm just trying to explain myself
So you can see the same picture

You may put me by myself,
And treat me like a loose thread
That needs to be pulled
But still you let me dangle

Does my dysgraphia upset you?
Does my handwriting make your life hard?
That I write with such free will and joy
Even if no one can understand it

Rising out of the lack of understanding
I'll try
To succeed in education
I'll try

I'm dysgraphic, dyslexic, eager and hopeful
Listening and learning in the flow of words
Overcoming prejudice and concepts
I'll try
Into classroom with technology making it clearer

I'll try
Thankful for Einstein, Picasso, Branson and others
Don't see it as a disadvantage, it's a different way of
thinking.
I'll try
I'll try
I'll try!

Meredith Marcolini (13)
West Buckland School, Barnstaple

YOUNG WRITERS INFORMATION

We hope you have enjoyed reading this book – and that you will continue to in the coming years.

If you're the parent or family member of an enthusiastic poet or story writer, do visit our website **www.youngwriters.co.uk/subscribe** and sign up to receive news, competitions, writing challenges and tips, activities and much, much more! There's lots to keep budding writers motivated!

If you would like to order further copies of this book, or any of our other titles, then please give us a call or order via your online account.

Young Writers
Remus House
Coltsfoot Drive
Peterborough
PE2 9BF
(01733) 890066
info@youngwriters.co.uk

JOIN IN THE CONVERSATION!

TIPS, NEWS, GIVEAWAYS AND MUCH MORE!

f YoungWritersUK

🐦 YoungWritersCW   📷 youngwriterscw

SCAN ME TO WATCH THE POWER OF POETRY VIDEO!